Best Practice Business Processes in the Supply Chain

Jutta Hasselmann

Copyright © 2013 Jutta Hasselmann

All rights reserved.

ISBN: 1492880051
ISBN-13: 978-1492880059

CONTENTS

Introduction		i
Some Notes		i
1	**Transportation**	1
	1.1 Freight Management	5
	1.2 Transport Planning and Dispatching	7
2	**Demand and Supply Planning**	11
	2.1 Demand Planning and Forecasting	11
	2.1.1 Demand Forecasting	11
	2.1.2 Demand Planning	13
	2.1.3 Demand Management	14
	2.2 Safety Stock Planning	18
	2.3 Supply Network Planning	19
	2.4 Distribution Planning	21
	2.5 Service Parts Planning	22
3	**Procurement**	25
	3.1 Strategic Sourcing	25
	3.2 Purchase Order Processing	28
	3.3 Purchase Order Processing Correction	29
	3.4 Procurement – Billing	31
4	**Manufacturing Collaboration**	35
5	**Warehousing**	37
	5.1 Inbound Processing and Receipt Confirmation	37
	5.2 Outbound Processing	38
	5.3 Cross Docking Planning	41
	5.4 Cross Docking Execution	41
	5.5 Storage Planning Inbound	43
	5.6 Storage Planning Outbound	44
	5.7 Storage Execution Inbound	45
	5.8 Storage Execution Outbound	46
	5.9 Physical Inventory Planning	47
	5.10 Physical Inventory Execution	49

6	**Order Fulfilment**		**51**
	6.1 Sales Order Processing		51
	6.2 Order Fulfilment – Billing		53
7	**Supply Chain Visibility**		**55**
	7.1 Strategic Supply Chain Design		55
	7.2 Supply Chain Analytics		56
	7.3 Supply Chain Risk Management		57
	7.4 Sales and Operations Planning		58

Introduction

The intention for this booklet is to give a complete end-to-end view on all the Supply Chain business processes without going into too much detail. In this sense the main objective is to clearly show what belongs to each business process and how the processes are interlinked without mixing them up.

The business processes are described in a way to provide the maximum practical usefulness for everyone who works in supply chain or whose work is in some way related to supply chain.

It should be noted that there are some limitations to business processes. Foremost of all is that the business processes can never substitute the necessary communication between relevant parties. It is important at all steps of the processes to have a list of the stakeholders and inform them regularly of any changes.

Some Notes

Some of the processes which are initiated within the Supply Chain business processes are themselves not Supply Chain business processes. They are only mentioned for completeness and not explained further within this booklet. These are the following higher level business processes:

Customer Contact to Solution (CC2S) - initiated in Strategic Sourcing and in Demand Management
Sales - initiated in Demand Management
Supplier Management - initiated in Demand Management
Quality Management - initiated in Demand Forecasting
Plan to Produce (P2P) - initiated in Sales Order Processing
Record to Report (R2R) - initiated in Procurement – Billing

Some industry specific Supply Chain business processes are not explained within this booklet, e. g. 'Service Parts Order Fulfilment', which is mostly used in the automotive industry.

In several business processes the warehouse staff performs certain activities. These could instead also be performed by a fully automated Warehouse Management System.

Some of the databases mentioned as data sources could be substituted with other data sources. The ERP system could also be substituted by other applications.

How the Supply Chain processes are interlinked is shown in the Process Landscape diagram which is available for download together with the Supply Chain business process diagrams at www.criticalea.com/supplychain.

1 TRANSPORTATION

The most important business process in the supply chain is Transportation. More specifically it is the 'Transport Planning and Dispatching' business process which is one of two Transportation business processes. 'Transport Planning and Dispatching' is the core of the supply chain which keeps all the other parts of the supply chain together. The other business process within Transportation is 'Freight Management'.

For the transportation of goods from its origin to its final destination, the freight could be transported by one or more transport modes. A transport mode is the type of transport used to transport the freight, e. g. rail, ship, lorry, barge. If there is only one transport mode used throughout the transportation, the term transmodal transportation is used. If several transport modes are used for the transportation, the term intermodal transportation is used.

Pure transmodal transportation, which means the freight is never reloaded throughout the complete route, does not happen often. Even if the same type of transport might be used throughout the transportation of the goods there will mostly be some transmodal operation required, e. g. a lorry delivers the goods to a distribution center, where the goods are unloaded and loaded onto another lorry for the remaining transport. This transmodal operation is called modal transloading.

An example for an intermodal transportation would be a lorry transporting freight to a rail terminal, where the freight is unloaded and then loaded onto a rail transport unit. In this case the intermodal operation is called intermodal transloading.

There are many different transloading facilities where goods can be transloaded, e. g. distribution centers, terminals, temporary storage facilities, rail yards.

In case of services, the terminology of delivery is used instead of transportation. Services are usually delivered by one delivery mode. In Information Technology supply chain the terminology of carriers is also used.

The Transportation Management is the business unit responsible for the 'Transport Planning and Dispatching' and the 'Freight Management' business processes. There is a vital difference between Transportation Management and Logistics. When a company uses Logistics Service Providers, it outsources the Transportation Management. In this case the transport orders which are issued by Transportation Management and which interlink many other business processes are not part of the company anymore. This leads to the fragmentation of the business processes in supply chain, usually causing many problems.

Transportation Management is indeed the one area that should not be outsourced as this leads to false economics and almost always to a heavy impact on profitability.

On the other hand the outsourcing of other business processes such as Demand Planning works quite well and should always be considered.

Most ERP systems do not understand the difference between Logistics and Transportation Management. This is the main reason why many companies do not use an ERP system for Transportation Management.

The 'Transport Planning and Dispatching' business process is interlinked with many other business processes (see Figure 1). The following business processes lead to the 'Transport Planning and Dispatching' process either directly or indirectly:

BEST PRACTICE BUSINESS PROCESSES IN THE SUPPLY CHAIN

- Distribution Planning
- Demand Planning
- Sales Order Processing
- Purchase Order Processing

The 'Transport Planning and Dispatching' process provides input to the following business processes:

- Inbound Processing and Receipt Confirmation
- Outbound Processing
- Cross Docking Planning
- Cross Docking Execution
- Storage Planning Inbound
- Storage Planning Outbound
- Storage Execution Inbound
- Storage Execution Outbound

The input it provides to these processes is indirect. Therefore there are no direct process interfaces in the 'Transport Planning and Dispatching' business process. However, it provides input to them e. g. in the form of Advanced Shipping Notification or transport orders which form the basis for these processes.

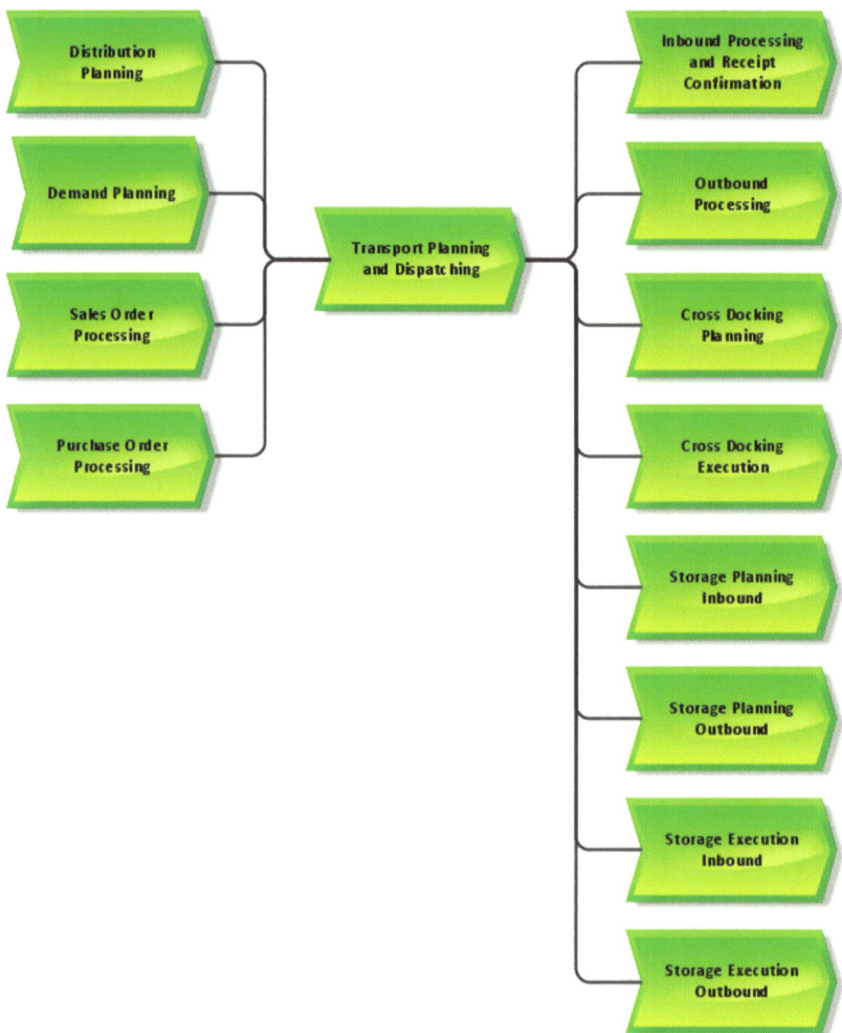

Figure 1

The 'Freight Management' business process is a prerequisite of the 'Transport Planning and Dispatching' and is therefore described first.

BEST PRACTICE BUSINESS PROCESSES IN THE SUPPLY CHAIN

1.1 Freight Management

This business process is triggered by the need to manage the transportation of goods from one location to another.

The following describes the business process in detail:

1. First, the geographic location of a destination has to be determined by Transportation Management. Factors such as the attachment to road network or the level of corruption are checked. Companies will not deliver to certain destinations mainly due to infrastructure access, distributors and corruption index. The Transportation system is used for this task.

    Considering all factors of the geographic location, it emerges if it is an acceptable destination or not.

    If the geographic location is acceptable, the Transportation Management enters the details in the Transportation System.

    If the geographic location is not acceptable, the Transportation Management informs the Demand Management. The process ends in this case for that particular location.

    The verification is often done via so-called Geographic Information Systems, which provide traffic information on all transport modes.

2. The Transportation Management allocates/creates freight codes for the goods destined for this destination in the Transportation System and in the ERP system.

    The freight codes indicate how the goods need to be transported, e. g. cooled, special security guarded. Special security would for example be necessary for the transport of medical narcotics or gold. It has to be noted that there are different freight codes for different destinations for the same goods.

3. The Transportation Management ascertains if goods require any special handling and/or if they belong to any hazard class. This information is entered in the Transportation System and the ERP

system. An example would be a toxic asset which is not allowed to be transported through certain areas. If the toxic asset is nuclear waste, then not only the areas to avoid would be important but the transport would also be subject to national security. In this case the management of the Transportation would need to be integrated with a national transportation system.

4. Also the maximum weight and dimension of the material unit is identified by the Transportation Management and entered in the Transportation System and the ERP system. An example of materials with opposing weight and volume are toilet paper and screws. If possible, in the 'Transport Planning and Dispatching' business process, materials like that are planned for the same transport in order to get the best possible mix.

5. The Transportation Management engages then in finding transport providers for certain geographic locations and transport modes.

    There are sometimes areas in which transport/delivery is not possible. Any of these Red List areas (in some countries also called black list areas) which the transport providers communicate will be taken into account and entered in the Transportation System by the Transportation Management.

6. From the collected transport providers the Transportation Management requests the transport unit price and information if the transport unit (e. g. container, bulk transport unit) is provided. The information is entered in the Transportation System.

    The transport unit price contains the price for the actual transport of the transport unit and the handling of it. The transport unit itself is not always provided by the transport provider. In this case the transport unit price would not include the price for the transport unit itself.

7. If the transport unit is not provided by the transport provider, which happens often, the Transportation Management engages in finding providers for transport units (e. g. container, bulk transport unit). Information is requested such as prices, minimum handling unit, if

stuffing is possible, how the transport unit can be returned. The data is entered in the Transportation System.

8. For intermodal and transmodal operations, transloading facilities (e.g. terminals, warehouses, distribution centers) are needed. Transportation Management engages in finding suitable transloading facilities, their prices and ascertains the duration for the intermodal/transmodal operation(s). The duration of intermodal/transmodal operations needs to be taken into account for correct planning of the transport modes. It should be noted that more often than expected one transloading facility costs more than everything else in the whole route.

9. The company might have its own transport facility or it solely uses transport providers. If it has its own transport facility, the Transportation Management compares the prices of the transport providers to its own transportation costs. The prioritization between the two is done with consideration of any prioritization policy in place.

10. The Transportation Management selects the most suitable transport providers and enters details in the Transportation System.

11. The transport providers inform Transportation Management of any required documents for certain goods which are entered in the Transportation System.

1.2 Transport Planning and Dispatching

Transport Planning and Dispatching is the core of the supply chain which keeps all the other parts of the supply chain together. If the Transport Planning and Dispatching does not work correctly then the whole supply chain will not function well leading to significant cost increases. For details please see the introduction of Transportation.

There is a continuous requirement for the planning of the transportation of goods in the supply chain.

The first step in transport planning is for Transportation Management to verify if the geographic location of the destination (GPS coordinates) is an accepted delivery location. If a geographic location is acceptable it is usually determined during Freight Management (see business process 'Freight Management') and is available in the Transportation System.

- If the geographic location is an accepted delivery location, the following activities occur:

    o Transportation Management identifies the types of transport by which the delivery location is accessible in the Transportation System.

    o Transportation Management checks if any mandatory way points are needed and gets the geographic locations for them from the Transportation System. Mandatory way points are locations, via which the goods have to be transported. These are often customs check points.

    o The following information is identified for the delivery:

        - the different material groups and how they have to be transported
        - if any special handling requirement/hazard classes apply
        - the quantity/weight/dimension of goods
        - the date and time for collection
        - the delivery date and time

    An example for goods with a special handling requirement is milk. It is categorized in the material group for dairy products with special handling requirement for transport. The reason is that spilled milk will develop into a slippery surface able to cause accidents.

    Transportation Management uses the ERP system and the Transportation System for this activity.

- o The Transportation Management then identifies possible transport providers, transloading facilities for the different material groups etc. using the Transportation System.

- o With all the gathered information at hand the route is planned considering all factors, e. g. costs, all intermodal transportation modes or transmodal transportation mode (all parts of the route if more than one) and operations, transloading facilities, duration for transloading. For example a warehouse would be necessary for an operation to store the delivered clothes collection for the following year until the delivery some months later.

  Transportation Management uses the ERP system and the Transportation System for this activity.

  It has to be noted, that warehouses are defined differently depending on their use.

- o The Transportation Management creates a transport order in the Transportation System for each mode of the route and transloading facility.

- o After the transport orders have been created, all required suppliers for all modes of the route and transloading facilites are selected. This is done taking into consideration the prioritization according to the prioritization policy. A supplier could be a company's own transport division.

  Transportation Management uses the Transportation System for this activity.

- o A purchase order is created for each of the suppliers of the modes of the route and transloading facilities. The purchase order(s) could be for a company's own transport division.

  Transportation Management uses the ERP system and the Transportation System for this activity.

- If the geographic location is not an accepted delivery location, the Transportation Management engages in resolving the conflict with the customer.

If no resolution is reached, which happens very seldom, there are no further activities regarding this particular transport planning and the process ends.

If the issue is resolved with the customer (goods will be delivered to a different destination), the process starts again with the verification of the new geographic location of the destination.

2 DEMAND AND SUPPLY PLANNING

2.1 Demand Planning and Forecasting

2.1.1 Demand Forecasting

This process is initiated by the requirement to forecast for a given future time period the quantities of products (stock keeping units = SKUs) to be produced and/or services to be offered. The forecast also includes the products and/or services which are required to produce the products and/or to provide the services.

The following describes the business process in detail:

1. The first decision point here is if the product or service is either new or not new.

    - If the product/service is new, there will naturally be no sales history and past forecast performance data available. In this case the similarity to other product(s)/service(s) is identified using proprietary or other data from e. g. seasonal and life cycle profiles. This activity is performed by the Demand Planner, the Sales and the Marketing Department using databases, e. g. Sales Database and Marketing Database.

    - If the product or service is not new and thus has been sold in the past, the Demand Planner and the Sales Department review the sales history and past forecast performance. The data are available in databases, e. g. Sales database, Demand and Forecast Data Database.

2. An unconstrained base volume forecast is then generated by the Demand Planner using the Demand and Forecast Data.

3. There are tangible events as well as intangible events which will or might happen during the time period for which the current forecast is done. These events will influence the demand of the products/services. Therefore, past demand shaping events are reviewed to understand their possible impact on the demand. This activity is performed by the Demand Planner, the Sales, Marketing and Finance Department using Sales and Marketing databases.

    There is the risk that certain events might not be under the Demand Planner's control, e. g.

    - Demand spikes due to promotions
    - Special event surges
    - Effects due to natural disaster

4. After the demand shaping events have been analyzed, the result will be used to fine-tune the forecast together with identified constraints and priorities. This is done by the Demand Planner using the Sales as well as the Demand and Forecast Data Databases.

    There are many risks for the quality of the forecast, some of which are:

    - Missing data integrity, e. g. multiple promotional SKUs for the same base product
    - Poor communication on changes in promotion mechanics
    - Internal collaboration and processes are inadequate to manage business and customer requirements. This often leads to double counting if the business unit managers do not see the larger picture.

5. The forecast is then finalized for performance measurement by the Demand Planner using the Demand and Forecast Data Database.

This process step initiates the business process 'Manufacturing Collaboration'.

There are many risks for the quality of the finalized forecast. Some of these risks are:

- Economic uncertainty can lead to extensive discrepancies between forecast figures and actual demand.
- If the forecast is too high, this will lead to higher inventory and therefore to higher costs.
- If the forecast is too low, this will lead to an increase in service level issues and therefore higher costs.

6. After the forecast is finalized, the quality of the product is defined by the Quality Manager, the Demand Planner, the Sales and the Marketing Department. The Sales and the Marketing Database are used for this task.

7. The quality of the product data is then managed by the Demand Planner using the Demand and Forecast Data Database. This role has the least vested interest and therefore manages the compromise between the different groups who defined the quality.

8. The Demand Planner makes the data available to the Quality Management which initiates the business process 'Quality Management'.

9. The forecast is evaluated after a certain time period by the Demand Planner applying a forecast error measurement methodology. After the analysis of the forecast error an action plan is created for forecast improvement.

2.1.2 Demand Planning

In the course of the period for which a forecast was made, the actual demand can prove to be different than forecasted. Thus the demand for the products/services has to be planned on a regular basis (e. g. monthly). According to the outcome of Demand Planning the forecast can then be adjusted if necessary.

The following describes the business process in detail:

1. First of all, the Demand Planner has to check with the Production Planning and with the Sales Department on any unforeseen events which are coming up or have already happened. For example the repair of production equipment is necessary and thus production cannot take place in a production hall or line. Or there could be a sudden surge of demand for products due to a natural disaster like an earthquake.

2. After checking if there are any unforeseen events, the actual Demand Planning takes place. The Demand and Forecast Data Database as well as the Stock system are used for the Demand Planning. This activity initiates the 'Safety Stock Planning' business process.

3. As a result of the Demand Planning an adjustment of the forecast might be necessary.

    If an adjustment of the forecast is necessary, the adjustment is done by the Demand Planner using the Demand and Forecast Data Database.

    It is important at all steps of the processes to have a list of the stakeholders and inform them regularly on any changes. E. g. Production is informed on the adjusted forecast.

    The demand data are then finalized by the Demand Planner using the Demand and Forecast Data Database and the ERP system.

4. After the Demand data has been finalized, the 'Distribution Planning' business process is initiated and the process ends.

2.1.3 Demand Management

Each day events can happen which potentially jeopardize the fulfilment of the demand. To ensure that demand can be met, daily Demand Management takes place. There are situations though, when a higher demand is not met, adhering to a certain strategy.

The daily events which might occur can be a higher customer demand than planned or a problem with supply/distribution or a problem in a production facility.

Each of these events with its ensuing activities is described in the following.

1. Higher customer demand than planned:

    Here the differentiation is necessary if the company produces the product/offers the service or is a reseller of the product/service.

    - If the company produces the product/service, one of two possible events happens. Either there is consent between the Sales and the Production Department to expand the Production or the Sales and/or the Production department decides against the expansion of the production.

        o If the Sales and the Production Department decide to expand the production, two parallel activities take place.

        The Demand Planner advises the responsible Production Manager to adjust the Production Plan. This initiates the business processes 'Manufacturing Collaboration' and 'Transport Planning and Dispatching'. The ERP system is used for this activity.

        The other activity is that a procurement order for products/services needed for the production is executed in the ERP system by either the Demand Planner or the Procurement Manager. Procurement is often done as a self-service in which case the Demand Planner would execute the procurement order without the involvement of the Procurement Manager. This activity initiates the 'Transport Planning and Dispatching' and the 'Distribution Planning' business processes.

- If the Sales and/or the Production Department decide against the expansion of the production, the higher customer demand will not be met. This could occur when the Sales Department decides that from a strategic viewpoint the production should not be extended at this point in time.

- If the company is a reseller of the product/service the Demand Planner consults the Sales Department if more products/services should be procured.

    - If the Sales department decides to procure additional products/services, the Demand Planner or the Procurement Manager executes a procurement order in the ERP system. Procurement is often done as a self-service in which case the Demand Planner would execute the procurement order without the involvement of the Procurement Manager.

        This activity initiates the 'Transport Planning and Dispatching' and the 'Distribution Planning' business processes.

    - The Sales department might decide against the procurement of further products/services e. g. because the products are promotional items and loss makers with the only purpose to bring market awareness.

2. Problem with supply/distribution:

    In this case a rule-based decision system decides on the criticality of the problem.

    - If the problem is a critical problem, there are two possible solutions. One solution is to order supply from another supplier by the Procurement Manager using the ERP system. This activity initiates the 'Supplier Management', 'Transport Planning and Dispatching' and 'Manufacturing Collaboration' business processes. The other solution is to manage the supply/distribution problem which is done by the Demand

Planner and the Transportation Manager using the ERP system. Sometimes drastic measures are taken, e. g. picking up a container by helicopter from a lorry stuck in traffic jam. This activity initiates the 'Transport Planning and Dispatching' business process.

- If the problem is non-critical, no further actions are required and the process ends.

3. Problem in production facility:

   In this case the solution depends on whether the company has another production facility or not.

   - If the company has another production facility, the Demand Planner contacts the Production Planner of the other production facility to determine if the production can be done at this plant.
     - If the production can be taken over by the other plant, the Demand Planner contacts the Controller and the Transportation Management to evaluate if the shipment costs are acceptable. The ERP system is used for the evaluation.
       - In case the shipment costs are acceptable, the Demand Planner informs the Production Planner that the shipment costs are acceptable and that therefore the production can be taken over by the Production Planner's plant. The Demand Planner also informs the Distribution Planner. The Production Planner adjusts the production plan, which could be part of the ERP system. The production plan is updated here since the loss of production could be long-term. The Distribution Planner adjusts the distribution planning in the ERP system.
       - In case the shipment costs are not acceptable, the Demand Planner informs the Sales and the Marketing department. The 'Sales' and the 'Customer Contact to

> > Solution (CC2S)' business processes are initiated here. The process ends.
>
> > o If the production cannot be taken over by the other plant, the Demand Planner informs the Sales and the Marketing department. The 'Sales' and the 'Customer Contact to Solution (CC2S)' business processes are initiated here. The process ends.
> >
> > A reason for the other plant not being able to take over production could be e. g. that the correct products for production or packaging for the products are not available at the other plant.
>
> - If the company does not have another production facility, the Sales and the Marketing department are informed by the Demand Planner. The 'Sales' and the 'Customer Contact to Solution (CC2S)' business processes are initiated here. The process ends.

2.2 Safety Stock Planning

The planning of safety stock is required on a regular basis to allow for variability of customer demand and other events. The Demand Planner uses the ERP system for the activities of this business process.

Safety stock of services is handled with a similar concept as safety stock of products. However, the planning of safety stock for services is to assign service staff on call. The time the service staff does not need for service calls they use for alternative work with lower priority.

The following describes the business process in detail:

1. The Demand Planner ascertains if the safety stock provision within the previous quarter was within predefined margin.

2. The findings show that the safety stock was either within the margin of +/- 20 % or outside of this margin for the previous quarter.

- If the safety stock was within the margin of +/- 20 %, the same safety stock is used for the new quarter.

- If the safety stock was outside the +/- 20 % margin, the Demand Planner adjusts the safety stock calculation in the ERP system.

  Every time a purchase order is executed, this calculation will add the safety stock on top.

2.3 Supply Network Planning

The Supply Network Planning is about the selection and evaluation of the right suppliers which has to be done on a regular predefined basis usually due to a renewal of a contract.

The following describes the business process in detail:

1. The Procurement Sourcer checks for alternative suppliers to the ones that are in the current Supply Network Model in the ERP system.

   Alternative suppliers are usually known to the Procurement Sourcer from the 'Strategic Sourcing' business process. Therefore no RFI is sent to potential suppliers within the 'Supply Network Planning' business process.

2. The Procurement Sourcer sends an RFP to alternative suppliers for evaluation. The evaluation criteria in the RFP are based on many attributes. The RFP used here is the RFP which was used in the Strategic Sourcing in the last contract cycle.

3. After receiving back the evaluations from the alternative suppliers, the Procurement Sourcer compares the alternative suppliers with the current suppliers based on chosen technique/criteria and selects the best suppliers. The comparison is based on e. g. quality, cost, flexibility, service etc.

4. All suppliers are contacted to inform of the outcome by the Procurement Sourcer, - the winning suppliers, the current suppliers and the suppliers which were not selected.

5. The Procurement Sourcer sends the contracts to the selected suppliers.

6. If the supplier does not agree with the contract, changes to the contract are negotiated between the supplier and the Legal Department and the Procurement Sourcer.

7. The supplier returns the signed contract to the Procurement Sourcer who enters it in the ERP system.

8. The Procurement Sourcer adjusts the Supply Network Model in the ERP system to reflect the chosen suppliers.

9. After the Supply Network Model is adjusted, the Procurement Sourcer checks if it matches the Demand Plan using the ERP system and the Demand and Forecast Data Database.

    - If the Supply Network Model and Demand Plan match, the Procurement Sourcer agrees the Supply Network Model with the suppliers.

    - If the Supply Network Model and Demand Plan do not match, the Procurement Sourcer adjusts the Supply Network Model and the process reverts back to when the Procurement Sourcer checks if the Supply Network Model and the Demand Plan match.

10. The Procurement Sourcer releases the Supply Network Model in the ERP system.

2.4 Distribution Planning

This business process is for the preparation of the information required for the 'Transport Planning and Dispatching' business process. It is initiated by the Demand Planning and the 'Demand Management' business processes.

The ERP system/Demand and Forecast Data database provides the following data required for this business process:

- Demand and Forecast Data for a future period
- Backordered demand at the end of a period
- Safety stock requirements for a future period
- Inventory level at the end of a period

The following describes the business process in detail:

1. The first activity for the Distribution Manager is to collect all identified items from the associated previous processes using the ERP system and the Demand and Forecast Data database.

2. The Distribution Manager identifies the inventory level of the items in the ERP system.

3. The total required quantity of each product is identified by the Distribution Manager, considering the back-orders and safety stock. The ERP system and the Demand and Forecast Data Database are used for this activity.

   The risk exists of a difference between the forecast and the actual demand, leading to an incorrectly identified quantity of required products.

4. The Distribution Manager identifies for each location, using the Demand and Forecast Data database and the ERP system:

   - which products are required
   - the required quantity of the products
   - the date/time when the products are required

This activity initiates the 'Manufacturing Collaboration' business process.

5. The Distribution Manager identifies when and where which product should be dispatched using the Demand and Forecast Data database and enters the information in the Transportation system.

   The following risks exist here:
   - Delays in supply and or lead time variability
   - Delays in conveying forecast changes to Distribution
   - Lack of synchronization between Distribution and Production or Marketing and Distribution.

2.5 Service Parts Planning

Service Parts Planning is required for revenue generation and the achievement of the legally mandated customer service level.

Some products have a clear life cycle whereas others do not. There are products that remain in fashion but others do not. This results in many different business processes for 'Service Parts Planning'. These processes are not necessarily wrong. They might be absolutely right for a certain industry.

The following description of the 'Service Parts Planning' business process is generalized for many different industries.

1. First of all the Demand Planner captures the demand history using the point of sale data.

2. Then the Demand Planner cleanses the demand history data.

3. After the data is cleansed it is validated. The Demand Planner uses the standard method of 'Outlier Correction' to validate the data.

4. The Demand Planner determines which products to forecast based on the statistical measure 'Covariance' and assigns a forecast code to these products. This activity is often done with statistical programs or spreadsheets.

5. The forecasting approach is chosen, which determines what groups and forecasting methods to use. The Demand Planner uses the Product Data History for this activity.

   The Demand Planner uses the Forecasting system for the following activities of grouping the products.

   A selection or all of the following groupings is prepared for forecasting:

   - Group products which can be forecast statistically.
   - Group products which will be forecast manually. These are products for which a statistical forecast is assumed to yield unsatisfactory results.
   - Group products which will be procured directly.
   - Group products which are in their end-of-life phase. These will be forecast either manually or based on a similar product's profile.
   - Group products which are in launch phase. These will be forecast either manually or based on a similar product's profile.
   - Group products for which the demand behaviour is known to the Demand Planner or that are high-value products. They will either be forecast manually or by standard forecasting method.

6. Then the Demand Planner makes the forecast for the products. It should be noted that the following is not an extensive list of possible forecasting methods.

   One or more of the following activities are performed, depending on which forecasting methods a company has chosen for its products:

   - The demand forecast is created by a manually selected forecasting method.

   - The demand forecast is created by an automatically selected forecasting method. Statistical tests are executed to ascertain the demand pattern for a product. These statistical tests are Trend Test, Seasonal Test, Intermittent Demand Test and error tests to choose between methods. The error tests determine the variance of the other tests and determine the result of the test with the best variance.

- The demand forecast is created based on the product life cycle.

7. It might be necessary to adjust the Demand Forecast based on active units of a particular product in the market. This is done to correct any statistical irregularity. The Demand Planner uses the Forecasting system for this activity.

8. The Demand Plan is then fine-tuned by the Demand Planner using the ERP system and the Forecasting system. This process step initiates the 'Purchase Order Processing' and the 'Transport Planning and Dispatching' business processes.

3 PROCUREMENT

3.1 Strategic Sourcing

Strategic Sourcing takes place if there is the need to open a new supply channel for a new strategic initiative. This could for example be the procurement of new products/services which have been tactically sourced before.

The Strategic Management Office informs the Procurement Department of any new required services and materials.

The following describes the business process in detail:

1. There are two activities which happen in parallel:

   - The Procurement identifies the products and services which the company procures, where they are procured from and their prices etc. to assess the company's current spending. The ERP system and the Sourcing Plan, which contains the specification and requirement of all services and materials, are used here.

   - The Procurement assesses any new materials and/or service requirements and stores the information in the Sourcing Plan.

2. The sourcing strategy is enhanced to accommodate any changes for the sourcing going forward. Changes could affect

- cost goals
- timing of when to start and end RFI, RFP, RFQ
- the weighting of RFI, RFP, RFQ for e. g.
  - guaranteed delivery times
  - guaranteed volume
  - guaranteed quality
  - price

Procurement uses the Sourcing Plan and the Cost Analysis spreadsheet for this activity.

3. Procurement looks for possible new suppliers.

4. After the selection of potentially qualified new suppliers has been made, Procurement sends these suppliers an RFI.

5. The contacted potential suppliers send their response back to Procurement.

6. The information received from the potential suppliers is then evaluated by Procurement and a credit/risk rating is done on these companies.

It has to be noted that apart from the credit/risk rating which is done on new potentially qualified suppliers, once a year an extensive credit/risk rating is done on all current suppliers to evaluate if they are viable. A supplier who produces something that cannot be procured anywhere else should be supported (e. g. joint venture).

7. The RFP/RFQ with technical specifications is prepared and the Sourcing Plan is adjusted if necessary. This is done by Procurement and other affected departments.

8. The Legal Department prepares the non-disclosure agreement for the potentially suitable suppliers. Procurement is involved in this activity. The non-disclosure agreement is then sent to the referring potential suppliers.

9. The contacted suppliers return the signed non-disclosure agreement to Procurement. If any changes were added from a supplier,

Procurement hands over the non-disclosure agreement to Legal Department to check on the changes.

This and the previous activity can happen repeatedly if any changes were made to the non-disclosure agreement.

10. Procurement contacts the potential suppliers with the RFP/RFQ with the technical specifications. The Sourcing Plan is used for this task.

11. The potential suppliers send their response to the RFP/RFQ to Procurement.

12. With all the responses received, Procurement then performs a total cost analysis to compare the cost of procuring those goods or services from different suppliers, the potential and the current suppliers, taking the Total Cost of Ownership (TCO) into account. The correspondence from current and potential suppliers, the ERP system and the Sourcing Plan is used here. A spreadsheet might be used as well.

13. Negotiation ensues between the Procurement and the suppliers on e. g. products, service levels, prices, geographical coverage etc. Procurement uses the Sourcing Plan for this activity.

14. After negotiation Procurement makes a temporary selection of suppliers.

15. Procurement then contacts the rejected suppliers to ascertain if they would like to renegotiate.

This and the previous activity can happen repeatedly until the potential suppliers have offered their final bid.

16. Procurement decides on which supplier(s) to use for certain products. Key stakeholders are involved in the decision process. The ERP system and the Sourcing Plan are used for this activity.

17. Procurement contacts all suppliers to inform them of the outcome, the winning suppliers, the suppliers which were not selected and the current suppliers if applicable.

18. The Legal Department sets up the contracts for the suppliers. Procurement is involved in this task as well. The Sourcing Plan is used for this activity.

19. Procurement sends the contracts to the suppliers.

20. If the supplier does not agree with the contract, changes to the contract are negotiated between the supplier and the Legal Department and Procurement.

21. The supplier returns the signed contract to Procurement.

22. Procurement enters the new strategic supplier contract details in the ERP system and the Sourcing Plan.

23. Procurement implements the new supply structure. For this activity the ERP system and the Sourcing Plan are used. Procurement informs key stakeholders of the supply structure changes.

    The 'Customer Contact to Solution (CC2S)' business process is initiated here.

3.2 Purchase Order Processing

This process is initiated by a purchase order in the ERP system. Purchase orders are usually generated automatically by the ERP system from the Demand Plan for products/services and the Demand Plan for service parts. Some purchase orders are entered manually in the ERP system, which is predominantly the case for services.

The following describes the business process in detail:

A Rule-based Decision system checks the order and decides if the order is accepted and thus can be processed automatically or if an exception occurs. The verification is done against the product catalogue, to see if it is part of the catalogue. The Rule-based Decision system also checks against other business rules, e. g. the order checks against a valid contract. All orders other than one-offs always need a contract. The reason is so that during contract negotiations all the foreseeable risks (e. g. supplier using child labour, financial risk) are excluded as well as that bulk payment terms are agreed.

The Product catalogue is created and edited in the 'Purchase to Pay' business process which is not part of the Supply Chain business process.

- If the purchase order is accepted by the Rule-based Decision system, the ERP system sends the order automatically to the supplier.

  This is called Operational Purchasing.

- If an exception occurs (e. g. no budget available) the following happens:

  The Purchasing Manager checks if the order is correct in the ERP system.

  If the order is correct, the Purchasing Manager flags the order as correct in the ERP system. The ERP system then sends the order automatically to the supplier.

  If the order is incorrect, the Purchasing Manager rejects the order in the ERP system and informs the person who placed the order to set up the order with the correct details. This initiates the 'Purchase Order Processing Correction' business process.

  This is called Tactical Purchasing.

3.3 Purchase Order Processing Correction

It is mostly a system related decision if an existing purchase order can be amended or a new purchase order is created. However, the budget could still prevent both of these options.

The following describes the business process in detail:

There are three possible scenarios:

1. The existing purchase order can be amended:

   This happens only in exceptional cases. The Purchase Manager checks the budget to evaluate if it permits the purchase order to be amended. The ERP system is used for this activity.

   Either the budget is available or it is not available:

   - If the budget is available the Purchasing Manager corrects the existing purchase order in the ERP system.

   - If the budget is not available, the Purchasing Manager rejects the change of the purchase order and adjusts the status of the purchase order in the ERP system.

     If the goods and/or services have already been delivered, they have to be returned to the supplier. This initiates the 'Transport Planning and Dispatching' business process for the return of goods and/or services to the supplier. If the goods and/or services have not yet been delivered, there are no goods and/or services to be returned. This could for example be the case when the purchase order has already been sent to the supplier, but the supplier could not deliver the goods or e. g. when the purchase order has not been sent to the supplier yet.

2. A new purchase order has to be created:

   The Purchase Manager checks the budget to evaluate if it permits the new purchase order to be created. The ERP system is used for this activity.

   Either the budget is available or it is not available:

   - If the budget is available, the Purchasing Manager deletes the old purchase order and creates a new purchase order in the ERP system. This initiates the 'Purchase Order Processing' business process.

- If the budget is not available, the exceeding part of any already delivered goods and/or services have to be returned to the supplier. This initiates the 'Transport Planning and Dispatching' business process for the return of goods and/or services to the supplier.

3. The purchase order is correct but there is a misunderstanding concerning the delivery:

In this case the Purchasing Manager renegotiates with the supplier to find a solution. The ERP system is used for this activity. Either the purchase order can then be amended or a new purchase order has to be created reverting to the beginning of this process.

This activity could also lead to escalation, which is handled differently in every company.

The Purchasing Manager contacts the supplier with the resolution.

3.4 Procurement – Billing

This business process is initiated either by the arrival of goods/provided services or the resolution of the 'Purchase Order Processing Correction' business process.

When goods arrive, the supplier is notified electronically by the shipping company of the receipt of goods at the customer site. With services the receipt is usually the worksheet or timesheet countersigned by the customer.

There are two possible methods for billing in the supply chain: the 3-way matching method, and invoiceless billing.

1. If the 3-way matching method is used for Billing the following activities take place:

    - The supplier sends the invoice with the referring purchase order number and a copy of the receipt of goods. If services were provided, a service receipt could for example be a monthly time sheet from a contractor.

- The ERP system checks if the purchase order number mentioned on the invoice matches with the purchase order. It also checks if the quantity of received items matches the quantity ordered in the purchase order.

    There are 3 different scenarios which can occur:

    o The purchase order number on the invoice cannot be matched to the purchase order.

    In this case the Account Payable Accountant and the supplier both check where the error lies, to ascertain if it is on the invoice or on the purchase order. The ERP system is used for this activity.

    - If the error is on the invoice, the AP Accountant rejects the invoice in the ERP system and requests the supplier to send a new invoice.

    - If the error is on the purchase order, the AP Accountant rejects the invoice in the ERP system and informs the Purchasing Manager. This initiates the 'Purchase order Processing Correction' business process.

    o The invoice amount or the quantity of the received items does not match the purchase order.

    The same applies as described in the above scenario.

    o The invoice amount and the received items match the purchase order or are lower than on the purchase order in case of a partial delivery.

    In this case the ERP system approves and initiates payment for the received goods/services. This triggers the 'Record to Report (R2R)' business process and once finished the 'Procurement Billing' business process ends.

2. If the Invoiceless Billing is used the following activities take place:

   The supplier sends a copy of the receipt and a copy of the purchase order. It could be that there are several receipts sent, in case purchase order line items can be invoiced on an individual basis. The ERP system processes these documents and checks if the purchase order number, the quantity and the product number match on the receipt(s) and the purchase order.

   - If the purchase order number, the quantity and the product number match on the receipt and the purchase order, the ERP system approves and initiates payment for the received goods and/or services.

   - If the purchase order number and the product number match on the receipt and the purchase order but the received quantity is lower than on the purchase order, the ERP system approves and initiates instalment for the received quantity of goods and/or services.

   In both of the above cases the 'Record to Report (R2R)' business process is triggered and once finished the 'Procurement Billing' business process ends.

   - If the purchase order number and/or the quantity and/or the product number do not match on the receipt and the purchase order, the ERP system sends notification to the supplier to inform about the error and rejects payment.

     This initiates the 'Purchase Order Processing Correction' business process.

4 MANUFACTURING COLLABORATION

This business process is initiated by the need to determine the manufacturing collaboration of material or in other words which material needs to be where and when for manufacturing.

This process is on the borderline of supply chain. It is often covered by the 'Production Planning (PP)' or 'Product Lifecycle Management (PLM)' business process instead of the Supply Chain business process.

The following describes the business process in detail:

The first activity is of the Production Manager to determine what material is allocated to the production site and which products have to be produced using the ERP system. The 'Distribution Planning' business process provides the information for this activity.

1. Material that will come into the production hall:

    The Production Manager breaks down the Bill of Material (BOM) into material numbers using the ERP system.

    After that the Production Manager determines if any discrepancy exists between the Bill of Material (BOM) and the Distribution Plan. If there is a discrepancy, the Production Manager informs the Demand Planner.

The Production Manager then determines which material numbers are needed when and at which locations (address, arrival dock, production line). The ERP system is used for this activity.

2. Material that will leave the production hall:

    The Production Manager lists material numbers for products that will leave the production hall using the ERP system.

    The Production Manager then determines which material numbers are needed when and at which locations (another production hall: address, arrival dock, production line; customer: address). The ERP system is used for this activity and the Transportation Management is involved.

The Production Manager sends the material numbers and allocation plan to the Transportation Management. The ERP system is used for this activity and the messages are usually sent in EDIFACT format.

5 WAREHOUSING

In the Warehousing business processes, the warehouse personnel are aware of the mode used to transport the goods to the warehouse and the mode used to transport from the warehouse. This helps in dealing with irregularities, e. g. a delayed delivery of next year's clothes collection to the warehouse would not cause any problems.

5.1 Inbound Processing and Receipt Confirmation

This business process is initiated by the receipt of an Advanced Shipping Notification (ASN) either from the supplier, Transportation Management or a logistics service provider containing the time of delivery, product description, quantities and packing information. It is also initiated when incorrect goods have been loaded during outbound processing.

The receipt of returned goods from a customer is not dealt within this business process concerning supply chain, although the unloading of returned goods takes place here. Return orders in this process relate to goods that have been incorrectly loaded.

The following describes the business process in detail:

1. Either an ASN is booked automatically against a purchase order or return order by the ERP system, or Warehouse Management books the ASN against the referring purchase order or return order. An ASN is booked against a return order for goods that have been

incorrectly loaded. It has to be noted that the receipt of returned goods from a customer is not dealt with in this process concerning supply chain.

2. The arrival of a certain quantity of goods at a certain date/time at a certain location takes place for either the production of own products, for cross-docking or for storage including any products which are for consumption. The arriving goods could also contain incorrectly delivered goods from the supplier. The warehouse staff unloads the arriving goods in any case. If the goods were sent by mistake from the supplier, the warehouse staff labels them for warehouse processing. The ERP system is used for this activity.

3. After the goods are in the receiving area, the Warehouse Management creates the goods receipt using the ERP system.

4. The ERP system posts the goods receipt in form of an EDIFACT message to the supplier. The supplier could also be the warehouse itself, in case the goods were loaded incorrectly.

5. At this point in time either the 'Storage Execution Inbound' or 'Cross Docking Execution' business process is initiated. For goods that have to be separated from a cross docking delivery, the business process 'Storage Execution Inbound' is initiated within the 'Cross Docking Execution' business process.

5.2 Outbound Processing

This business process is initiated by transport orders which are available from Transportation Management for shipment of goods from the warehouse, e. g. based on a sales order or a stock transfer order.

The following describes the business process in detail:

1. First of all, the Warehouse Management prepares the outbound delivery based on the transport orders received from Transportation Management. The ERP system is used for the preparation of the outbound delivery.

2. The Warehouse Management then checks the outbound delivery against storage and/or cross docking documentation using the ERP system.

   If the outbound delivery, storage and cross docking documentation do not match, Warehouse Management contacts Storage and Cross Docking for resolution. In this case the process flows back to preparing the outbound delivery based on the transport orders.

3. The Warehouse Management creates warehouse tasks using the ERP system.

4. When the outbound delivery is due, either the goods are at the staging area or they are at the outbound delivery dock, having been transferred straight through for cross docking.

5. If products have to be picked, the warehouse staff picks the relevant products. The ERP system is used for this activity.

   This activity and the following could be completely automated using RFID tags or barcodes.

6. Either the products are already packed as required by the transport order or they have to be packed in handling units.

   - If the products are already packed according to the transport order, the warehouse staff prints labels and/or RFID tags using the ERP system and labels the handling units.

     The labelling can happen at the outbound delivery dock or even in the transport unit.

   - If the products have to be packed in handling units, the warehouse staff packs them according to the transport order. The ERP system is used for this activity.

     The warehouse staff prints labels and/or RFID tags using the ERP system and labels the handling units.

7. The warehouse staff produces loading papers and, if required, export papers using the ERP system.

8. The warehouse staff loads the goods onto vehicles/transport units according to the sequence specified in the transport order. The ERP system is used and the transport staff is involved in this activity.

   It has to be noted that there is a transport order for each transport unit used in an outbound delivery.

9. The warehouse tasks are confirmed in the ERP system by the warehouse staff.

10. The transport staff either confirms or declines accuracy of the loaded handling units to the warehouse staff.

    In case the transport staff disapproves of the accuracy of the loaded handling units, there can be three different scenarios of what happened. One is that one or more handling units have been loaded by mistake. The other is that a handling unit has not been loaded. And the third is that one or more handling units have been loaded by mistake instead of alternative handling unit(s).

    - If one or more handling units have been loaded by mistake, the warehouse staff unloads the mistakenly loaded handling units, and enters details in the ERP system which creates an Advanced Shipping Notification for the excess goods. The 'Inbound Processing and Receipt Confirmation' business process is initiated here. The process reverts to when the Transport staff either confirms or declines accuracy of the loaded handling units.

    - If a handling unit has not been loaded, the process reverts to when the Warehouse Management creates warehouse tasks.

    - If one or more handling units have been loaded instead of the correct ones, the warehouse staff unloads the mistakenly loaded handling units and enters details in the ERP system which creates an Advanced Shipping Notification. The warehouse staff creates warehouse task(s). The 'Inbound Processing and Receipt Confirmation' business process is initiated here. The process reverts to where the goods are either at the staging area or at the outbound delivery dock.

11. When the vehicle(s)/transport units have left the yard, the warehouse staff posts the goods issue in the ERP system and sets the outbound delivery as complete. This updates the inventory.

12. The ERP system sends the Advanced Shipping Notification to the customer in the form of an EDIFACT message.

5.3 Cross Docking Planning

This business process is initiated by Transportation Management issuing transport orders which contain transfer orders for cross docking.

Based on these transport orders, the Warehouse Management plans the cross docking with details such as the gates which will be used for inbound and outbound processing and the staging areas, using the ERP system. The priority of goods is taken into account during planning. The Cross Docking details document is created during this task.

The Warehouse Management informs the Transportation Management or if Transportation Management is outsourced the Logistics Service Provider of gates for inbound and outbound deliveries. The Cross Docking details document and the ERP system is used for this task.

5.4 Cross Docking Execution

This business process is initiated by arriving goods which are flagged for cross docking in a transport order.

These goods have to be either transferred directly to another dock, or they have to be brought to a staging area.

1. If the goods have to be transferred directly to another dock, the warehouse staff transports these goods to the indicated outbound delivery dock. This triggers the 'Outbound Processing' business

process, and once finished the 'Cross Docking Execution' process ends.

2. If the goods have to be brought to a staging area first, the warehouse staff transports these goods to the staging area.

   There are different scenarios for what happens regarding these goods at the staging area. These scenarios are explained in the following sections:

   - The products do not need to be repackaged. This can happen if the products have to be brought to a staging area and remain there until they can be loaded. In this case the 'Outbound Processing' business process is triggered, and once finished the 'Cross Docking Execution' process ends.

   - Goods have to be split into different handling units. This task is done by the warehouse staff. This triggers the 'Outbound Processing' business process, and once finished the 'Cross Docking Execution' process ends. The ERP system is used here.

   - Goods have to be split for storage from goods for cross docking. This task is undertaken by the warehouse staff. This initiates the 'Storage Execution Inbound' business process for the goods that are not for cross docking. It also triggers the 'Outbound Processing' business process for the cross docking goods, and once this process is finished the 'Cross Docking Execution' process ends. The ERP system is used here.

   - Goods from storage have to be added to goods for cross docking at the staging area. This triggers the 'Outbound Processing' business process and once finished the 'Cross Docking Execution' process ends.

5.5 Storage Planning Inbound

This business process is initiated by transport orders from Transportation Management which specify that certain goods which will arrive have to be stored in the warehouse. All activities are performed by the Warehouse Management.

1. The Warehouse Management consults the expected receipts from the transport orders and current backlogs in the ERP system and identifies the required storage space.

2. Possible storage locations for the goods are identified taking into account e. g. dimension capacity, carrying capacity, storing conditions, frequency of access, and proximity to other products etc. The ERP system and the Warehouse Logistics system are used for this activity.

3. After that the physical storage locations for the goods are planned. The ERP system and the Warehouse Logistics system are used for this activity.

4. The storage locations are then reserved for the expected goods. The ERP system and the Warehouse Logistics system are used for this activity.

5. Two parallel activities then occur. Firstly, the timing and priority of inbound and outbound access to storage locations is planned in order to prevent congestion. This is also done to adhere to certain timing of special storage locations, e. g. a safe for toxic goods which can only be opened at certain times per day. Secondly, travel time to the storage location is managed by planning the best travel routes. The ERP system and the Warehouse Logistics system are used for these activities.

6. Several possible outcomes can occur from the storage planning in terms of what will happen with the goods on arrival, and can be one, or a combination of the following:

    - Certain goods have to be delivered to staging area(s) before they can be stored in the warehouse.

- Certain goods have to be stored directly.
- Goods with specific storage instructions have to be stored in special intermediary location before they can be stored at their final storage location.

7. The Warehouse Management then creates the warehouse tasks. The ERP system is used for this activity.

5.6 Storage Planning Outbound

This business process is initiated by transport orders from Transportation Management which specify the details for outbound deliveries. All activities are performed by the Warehouse Management.

The following describes the business process in detail:

1. The Warehouse Management determines, if the goods to be shipped have an expiry date. The ERP system is used for this activity.

2. The goods handling instructions for the warehouse task(s) are prepared. If the goods have an expiry date, then the instructions will include selecting the goods first that expire earlier.

3. Two parallel activities then occur. Firstly to plan the timing and priority of inbound and outbound access from the storage locations to prevent congestion in the warehouse and to adhere to any specific timing of special storage locations. E. g. a safe for toxic goods can only be opened at certain times per day. Secondly to manage travel times from the storage locations by planning of best travel routes. The ERP system and Warehouse Logistics system are used for both of these activities.

4. The outcome of the planning shows if the goods have to be delivered to staging area(s) before loading or if goods with special storage instructions have to be loaded directly.

5. The Warehouse Management creates the warehouse tasks using the ERP system.

5.7 Storage Execution Inbound

This business process is initiated by the receipt of goods which are flagged in the warehouse task for storing in the warehouse.

The warehouse task(s) could either be available in the form of a document or on a tablet computer.

It has to be noted that the following activities could happen automatically, in which case the handling unit has an RFID or barcode identifier.

The following describes the business process in detail:

1. Among the arriving goods could be returned goods for various reasons, e. g. defective goods. In this case the warehouse staff labels them as defective, using the ERP system for this task.

   Defective products are handled as normal products from the warehouse perspective. However, instead of shipping the products e. g. to a customer, they are shipped to recycling/repair in the 'Outbound Processing' business process.

   The eligibility of return is checked on any returned goods. After that the goods receipt is created for the returned goods. The warehouse staff uses the ERP system for both of these activities. The goods receipt for other arriving goods which are not returned goods has already been created in the 'Inbound Processing and Receipt Confirmation' business process.

2. Either the warehouse staff transports the goods from the receiving area to a staging area or they transport them directly to their storage location according to the warehouse task(s).

3. For goods that have been transported to a staging area, the warehouse task could indicate that they have to be split in different handling units. If this is the case, the warehouse staff splits the goods in the handling units indicated in the warehouse task. The warehouse task could also indicate that these goods have specific handling instructions, e. g. the goods have to be stored cooled until

cross docking can continue. The warehouse staff adheres to any handling instructions given in the warehouse task and prepares the storage location if required. Any preparation requirement would also be indicated in the warehouse task.

There can be other reasons for bringing the goods to the staging area first before storing them away, e. g. timing for storing away has to be adhered to in order to avoid congestion, or to open a certain storage location at its permitted time.

The warehouse staff transports the goods from the staging area to their storage location specified in the warehouse task.

4. The warehouse staff creates the storage receipt in the ERP system.

5.8 Storage Execution Outbound

This business process is initiated by the warehouse task instructing the transportation of goods from their storage location to a designated location.

The warehouse task(s) could either be available in the form of a document or on a tablet computer.

The following describes the business process in detail:

1. The warehouse staff picks the goods from the storage location adhering to any special handling instructions as stated in the warehouse task(s).

2. The goods are then delivered by the warehouse staff to the designated location adhering to any special handling instructions as stated in the warehouse task(s).

3. There might only be part of the goods on a handling unit (e. g. pallet) required for the outbound delivery. In this case the picking of the required quantity of goods is done as part of the 'Outbound Processing' business process. After the picking is undertaken the

warehouse staff transports the excess goods back to their storage location as indicated in the warehouse task(s).

4. The warehouse staff confirms the warehouse task(s) in the ERP system.

5.9 Physical Inventory Planning

This business process is initiated by the requirement to plan the periodic counting of the inventory. Note: Although this business process is very important, most managers shun getting involved in this process as it is usually considered quite boring.

The following describes the business process in detail:

1. The Warehouse Management chooses a method to conduct a physical inventory. The method could either be the counting with barcode readers, with count (index) cards with information and location of individual products or with pre-printed lists of inventory for a hand count.

   It has to be noted that the use of RFID readers is not recommended for untertaking a physical inventory. The reason is that sometimes RFID tags are laying around somewhere, but the goods have been stolen, which would lead to a false inventory count.

2. The Warehouse Management then decides on whether slow moving items will be counted and marked a day before the full inventory takes place.

3. After that, the Warehouse Management updates the Inventory Plan and Instructions with the date(s) and time(s) of the next physical inventory, the assigned responsible persons, the method of counting, the process of recording and reconciliation, any unknown items, the auditor's approval requirements etc.

The date(s) and time(s) should be scheduled for quieter periods of the business operations. The inventory counting might take place on different days in case there are several remote warehouses.

It is best practice to inform the suppliers of the date and time of the inventory.

There could be more than one counting method selected, e. g. one method for finished goods and another method for work-in-process (WIP) or for raw materials.

4. Two parallel activities then follow. The Warehouse Management publishes the Inventory Plan and Instructions and informs the relevant personnel, who has been assigned as responsible for the next physical inventory.

5. The Warehouse Management selects the relevant employees for counting, forms counting team(s) and informs those selected.

6. The Health & Safety Officer and the Warehouse Management provide Health & Safety equipment for all team members who will conduct the next physical inventory.

7. Training of selected employees might be performed on material types, counting method(s) and documentation. Warehouse Management conducts the training.

8. The employees prepare the warehouse before the physical inventory. They ensure that all goods are in the correct place and can be clearly identified. They also make sure that the storage area is cleaned and that all shelves and locations are labelled.

9. The employees identify any damaged, discounted and discontinued items and place them separately from other inventory to be written off.

10. The employees prepare and provide the stock location plan.

5.10 Physical Inventory Execution

This business process is initiated by the requirement to conduct a physical inventory at a certain date, time and location. The task of performing a physical inventory could also be outsourced.

The following describes the business process in detail:

1. The whole or part of the business operations and inventory transactions are stopped on the day of the physical inventory according to the Inventory Plan and Instructions. The Warehouse Management and Auditor are the responsible people for this activity.

2. The Auditor and the Warehouse Management assign tasks to the employees who will conduct the physical inventory ensuring that each employee who supervises or performs a count is an independent person in the assigned task so that no employee supervises or counts areas for which he or she is directly responsible.

3. The Auditor and the Warehouse Management ensure that the employees who will conduct the count have no access to current inventory quantities recorded in the accounting records, in order that the count will be a blind count.

4. For the counting of the inventory a certain method is preselected as part of the 'Physical Inventory Planning' business process. Either count cards, lists or barcode readers are used.

   - If count cards or lists are used, the Warehouse Management and the Auditor number these sequentially and hand them out to the employees.

   The employees then conduct the count and measure goods if applicable according to the inventory policy in the Inventory Plan and Instructions. The counted and measured goods are marked as counted and recorded in the count cards or lists.

   The employees sign the count cards or lists they have used to record the counted goods and hand them back to the Auditor and Warehouse Management. Any empty count cards or lists are handed back as well.

The Warehouse Management and the Auditor check that all the count cards or lists have been returned.

- If barcode readers are used for the count, the Warehouse Management and the Auditor hand these over to the employees and record to whom each device was given.

    The employees then conduct the count and measure goods if applicable according to the inventory policy in the Inventory Plan and Instructions. The counted and measured goods are marked as counted.

    After the count is done, the employees hand back the barcode readers to Warehouse Management and the Auditor.

5. The assigned employees enter the counts from the count cards, lists or barcode readers in the ERP system. These cannot be the same employees who count the inventory items.

6. The Auditor then cross-references the counts with the accounting records in the ERP system.

7. Two parallel activities then happen. The Auditor audits the counts and creates an Audit report and the Warehouse Management reorders the goods of which the actual inventory is smaller than the accounting figures using the ERP system.

8. If the deviation of the counts from the accounting records is greater than the defined threshold, then the Auditor escalates the issue. This could lead to a recount.

    A deviation from the accounting records within the defined threshold is acceptable.

6 ORDER FULFILMENT

6.1 Sales Order Processing

This business process is initiated by the receipt of a purchase order from a customer.

Usually this process is not covered by supply chain and is only documented here in its basic form to ensure that the overall Supply Chain processes can be followed through.

The following describes the business process in detail:

1. Either the ERP system sets up the buyer details initiated by self-service of the purchase order or the Sales Department enters the buyer details into the ERP system.

2. The Sales Department enters or checks (if the sales order is already created by self-service of the purchase order) the sales order in the ERP system. If there is a previously issued quotation which led to this sales order, it is referenced in the sales order.

    This activity is often automatically performed by the ERP system.

3. Either the product(s) need to be configured/assembled or not.

    - If the product(s) need to be configured/assembled, the Sales Department enters the details of the configuration/assembly of products in the sales order in the ERP system. This initiates the 'Plan to Produce (P2P)' business process.

- If the product(s) do not need to be configured/assembled, the Sales Department enters the product(s) in the sales order in the ERP system.

4. The ERP system then performs a credit check on the customer. If the credit check is negative, the Sales Department informs the customer of the negative credit check. This is often automatically performed by the ERP system. Either the customer then makes a prepayment of the ordered product(s) or in case of no prepayment the sales order is flagged in the ERP system as not executable and the process ends.

5. The Sales department checks in the ERP system if the product(s) are available and schedules them for delivery. In case the products are not in stock, a predefined delivery time in the future is determined. The customer is then advised of that delivery date.

If the product(s) are not in stock the following activities happen:

- The Sales department creates a backorder in the ERP system.

- The Demand Planner then checks in the ERP system if the products are scheduled for reordering in the Demand Plan.

In case there is no reordering scheduled in the Demand Plan, the Sales department creates a purchase order for the product(s) in the ERP system.

The Sales department keeps the backorder on the ERP system until the expected delivery time. The process reverts to when the Sales department checks if the product(s) are available and schedules the product(s) for delivery.

6. The Sales department processes the sales order in the ERP system. This initiates the 'Transport Planning and Dispatching' business process.

7. The Sales department sends the order confirmation to the customer using the ERP system. This is often automatically performed by the ERP system.

8. The Sales department monitors the status of the order in the ERP system.

6.2   Order Fulfilment – Billing

This business process is initiated when the products are shipped to the customer.

Either the customer has pre-paid the products or the products are not paid yet.

1. If the customer has pre-paid the products, the ERP system issues the invoice for the referring purchase order indicating the status and the mode of payment. The ERP system sends the invoice automatically to the customer.

2. If the products are not prepaid, the Accounts Receivable Accountant issues the invoice for the referring purchase order in the ERP system. This is often automatically performed by the ERP system. The ERP system sends the invoice automatically to the customer. This initiates the 'Accounts Receivable' business process.

7 SUPPLY CHAIN VISIBILITY

7.1 Strategic Supply Chain Design

This business process is initiated regularly (e. g. monthly) to increase revenue and improve customer service.

The following describes the business process in detail:

1. There are two sets of activities which are performed in parallel:

    - One set of activities are the following:

      The Controller performs activity based costing in comparing invoices and other costs against activities. A Data Warehouse is used for this activity.

      Then the Controller analyses the activities with very high costings, usually done with a spreadsheet, to find ways to lower costs. This is called tactical cost cutting.

      After that the Supply Chain Management and the Controller create recommendations for cost efficiency. It has to be noted that sometimes the overall costs of the supply chain are reduced by increasing the costs in an area, e. g. more expensive packaging for easier handling.

- The other set of activities are the following:

    The Supply Chain Management uses a Data Warehouse to determine the process times and compare them against the Service Level Agreements (SLAs).

    If the process time is longer than agreed in the SLA, then the Supply Chain Management takes measures to get the process time within the SLA.

2. The Controller and the Supply Chain Management create a Visibility Report on the findings which is then distributed to the relevant parties.

7.2 Supply Chain Analytics

On a regular basis, supply chain analytics have to be provided to ensure that the decisions in the enterprise are made on present facts.

The following describes the business process in detail:

1. First of all, the Business Partner Management gathers all Critical Success Factors (CSFs) in the enterprise and from other sources, e. g. customers and suppliers.

    All the CSFs are gathered on a periodic basis to avoid scope creep of unnecessary reports. The entities which could require a CSF report are vast and therefore not listed. To give an example, however, this could be a government or an environmental agency.

2. The Data Owner and the Data Architect identify the data which is required to create reports on the CSFs.

3. The Data Architect checks if all the required data is available in the Data Warehouse.

    - If all data is available for Online Analytical Processing (OLAP), the Data Owner initiates a request for change to the IT department to design and implement the analytics.

The IT Department and the Data Architect then design and implement the analytics in the Data Warehouse.

After implementation, the Project Manager informs the relevant parties that the analytics are available.

- If not all data is available for OLAP, the Data Owner informs the Business Project Manager and the IT Project Manager about the combined change request to gather the missing data.

    o If the data can be gathered, the IT department implements the combined change to acquire the missing data. The process reverts back to when the Data Architect checks if all required data is available.

    o If the data cannot be gathered, the Data Owner informs the relevant parties that the report is not possible and the process ends.

7.3 Supply Chain Risk Management

On a regular basis, risk analytics have to be provided to ensure that the decisions in the enterprise are made on present facts.

The following describes the business process in detail:

1. First of all the Business Risk Manager gathers all the Critical Risk Factors (CRFs) in the enterprise and from other sources, e. g. customers and suppliers.

    All the CRFs are gathered on a periodic basis to avoid scope creep of unnecessary reports. The entities which could require a CRF report are vast and therefore not listed. To give an example, however, this could be a government or an environmental agency.

2. The Data Owner and the Data Architect identify the data which is required to create reports on the CRFs.

3. The Data Architect checks if all the required data is available in the Data Warehouse.

   - If all data is available for Online Analytical Processing (OLAP), the Data Owner initiates a request for change to the IT department to design and implement analytics.

     The IT Department and the Data Architect then design and implement the analytics in the Data Warehouse.

     After implementation, the Project Manager informs the relevant parties that the analytics are available.

   - If not all data is available for OLAP, the Data Owner informs the Business Risk Manager and the IT Project Manager about the combined change request to gather the missing data.

     o If the data can be gathered, the IT department implements the combined change to acquire the missing data. The process reverts back to when the Data Architect checks if all required data is available.

     o If the data cannot be gathered, the Business Risk Manager informs the relevant parties that the report is not possible. The process ends.

7.4 Sales and Operations Planning

This business process is initiated on a regular predefined basis by the necessity to report on customer analytics for operational and sales planning. The activities for both occur in parallel.

The following describes the business process in detail:

1. For operations planning, a System Analyst gathers all support tickets from the Customer Service System and selects the supply chain related ones.

BEST PRACTICE BUSINESS PROCESSES IN THE SUPPLY CHAIN

   The System Analyst then creates reports on the supply chain related tickets using the Customer Service System.

2. For sales planning, a System Analyst gathers data on past delivery problems from the Data Warehouse and from various other systems. Delivery problems could be issues such as late delivery or incorrect product delivery.

   The System Analyst then creates a report on problems of individual key customers. The Data Warehouse is used for this activity.

   The Sales force contacts the key customers to gather data on lost revenue due to delivery problems.

   The System Analyst creates the lost revenue report against supply chain problems by key customer using the Data Warehouse.

3. The Operations and the Sales report are then distributed by the System Analyst to the relevant parties.

www.ingramcontent.com/pod-product-compliance
Lightning Source LLC
Chambersburg PA
CBHW040841180526
45159CB00001B/274